JOHN WESLEY'S

HEART-WARMING

RELIGION

by

J. C. McPheeters

First Fruits Press
Wilmore, Kentucky
c2012

ISBN-13:9781621710042

John Wesley's Heart-Warming Religion, by J. C. McPheeters.
First Fruits Press, © 2012
Pentecostal Publishing Company, © 1900

Digital version at
http://place.asburyseminary.edu/firstfruitsheritagematerial/12/

First Fruits Press is a digital imprint of the Asbury Theological Seminary, B.L. Fisher Library. Asbury Theological Seminary is the legal owner of the material previously published by the Pentecostal Publishing Co. and reserves the right to release new editions of this material as well as new material produced by Asbury Theological Seminary. Its publications are available for noncommercial and educational uses, such as research, teaching and private study. First Fruits Press has licensed the digital version of this work under the Creative Commons Attribution Noncommercial 3.0 United States License. To view a copy of this license, visit http://creativecommons.org/licenses/by-nc/3.0/us/.

For all other uses, contact:

First Fruits Press
B.L. Fisher Library
Asbury Theological Seminary
204 N. Lexington Ave.
Wilmore, KY 40390
http://place.asburyseminary.edu/firstfruits

McPheeters, J. C. (Julian Claudius), 1889-1983.
   John Wesley's heart-warming religion / by J.C. McPheeters.
   Wilmore, Ky. : First Fruits Press, c2012.
   Reprint. Previously published: Louisville, Ky. : Pentecostal Publishing Company, [194-?].
   ISBN: 9781621710042
   1. Methodism -- History. 2. Wesley, John, 1703-1791. I. Title.
BX8231 .M36 2012

Cover design by Haley Hill

asburyseminary.edu
800.2ASBURY
204 North Lexington Avenue
Wilmore, Kentucky 40390

First Fruits
THE ACADEMIC OPEN PRESS OF ASBURY SEMINARY

John Wesley's

HEART-WARMING

Religion

By J. C. McPheeters, D.D.

President, Asbury Theological Seminary.

PENTECOSTAL PUBLISHING COMPANY
LOUISVILLE, KENTUCKY.

CONTENTS

Strangely Warmed Heart 5
The Failure of Good Works 6
Wesley Meets Peter Bohler 8
The Heart Warming Testimony 11
On Sanctification 13
A Distinguished Theologian On Wesley's Views 14
Two Epochs in Christian Experience 17
Mixed Holiness 20
Justification and Sanctification 21
Early Methodists and the Warmhearted Experience 23
Justification and Sanctification by Faith 25
Without Faith Nothing Avails 26
When May the Christian Be Sanctified? 28
Another Noted Theologian Interprets
Wesley's Views 30
The Test of Scriptural Argument and
    Modern Scholarship 32
The Ultimate Stroke 34
A Noted Theologian Answers Objections 36
Obtainable In This Life 38
A Major Emphasis of Early Methodists 40
The Interpretation of Wesley's Position 44
Sanctification May Come In A Moment 46
Perfect Love In Complete Control 47
Wesley Maintains His Position to the End 48
Did Wesley Profess the Experience? 50
Snowsfields: A Great Epoch Similar to Aldersgate 51
No Finality In Perfection 53
"Still Breathing Nothing But Love" 55
The Time and Manner of Receiving Perfect Love .. 59
A Passionate Plea 61
A Living Sacrifice 63

The Strangely Warmed Heart

John Wesley's religion of the strangely warmed heart has wielded a world-wide influence. It was the birth of a mighty revival which transformed England, and spread to the regions beyond, until every continent of the earth felt the impact of it.

An epochal experience came to John Wesley on May 24, 1738, which he describes in these words:

"In the evening I went very unwillingly to the society in Aldersgate Street, where one was reading Luther's preface to the Epistle to the Romans. At about a quarter before nine, while he was describing the change which God works in the heart through faith in Christ, I felt my heart strangely warmed. I felt I did trust in Christ, Christ alone, for salvation; and an assurance was given me, that he had taken away my sins, even mine, and saved me from the law of sin and death."

John Wesley was, at that time, 35 years of age, and he was no novice in matters pertaining to religion and ecclesiastical affairs. He was a collegiate in every sense of the word. He held a Master's degree from the University of Oxford, and was a Fellow of that historic university. He was an ordained priest of the Established Church of England, and had been preaching thirteen years.

Not only had he been a minister for this length of time, but he had been a missionary to America, where he spent nineteen months preaching the gospel in and about the environs of Savannah, Georgia. At Savannah he endured many hardships, and gave himself unstintedly to his missionary task. John Wesley was trained in matters of theology. He was not a bad man who needed moral reformation, but he did need the strangely warmed heart.

The Failure of Good Works

Previous to Aldersgate John Wesley said that he hoped to be saved, "by not being as bad as some people, having a kindness for religion, reading the Bible, going to church, and saying my prayers". In that period preceding Aldersgate, although an indefatigable preacher and religious worker, he knew not the experience of the strangely warmed heart. While John Wesley had the advantage of the best schools of his day, and was a scholar, he failed to find in his scholastic attainments an answer to the craving that his heart desired. Scholarship without the strangely warmed heart is cold, dead and formal, and makes little imprint on the world for human redemption.

Mr. Wesley also had as the background of his scholarship a splendid home training. Susannah Wesley is recognized as one of the great women of history. She was the mother of nineteen children, and conducted a school for her children in her home. The systematic manner in which Susannah Wesley trained her children stands as a marvel to this day.

We cannot lay too much emphasis upon the significance and the far reaching influence of proper home training. It is one of the things sadly lacking in this age with its loose morals and its lack of discipline in the home. But splendid home training cannot satisfy the inner cry and cravings of the human heart.

When parents are all that could be demanded, in the matter of giving the child proper training, such parents cannot satisfy the needs of the human heart.

There is a cry in the heart for something more than learning, more than the intimate friendships and relationships of the best ordered family. John Wesley, with his excellent home training and splendid university training, had a yearning for an inner satisfying heart experience with God.

John Wesley had no conception of the possibility of his heart being changed in a moment, He set about to satisfy the deep longing and craving of his heart for peace and rest, by turning to good works. He undertook to obtain the experience for which his heart desired by being a good man, and the doing of good deeds.

One of Wesley's first steps in his program of good works was to become a preacher. From Oxford he went to Epworth, where he began his preaching. In his early ministry he struck no fire in his preaching. Writing of that period in his ministry Mr. Wesley said: "I preached much, but saw no fruits of my labors."

There was nothing stirring or gripping in Wesley's ministry previous to his heart warming experience. There was nothing extraordinary about it. There were no conversions under his preaching. In describing his own condition he said: "I dragged on heavily." He did his work through a sense of duty without any spontaneous compulsion that fired his heart from within.

John Wesley's zeal in giving attention to good works

carried him, as a missionary, across the Atlantic to America. While on board ship enroute to America he wrote in his journal: "Why am I going to America?" He answered as follows: "My chief motive is the hope of saving my own soul. I hope to learn the true use of the Gospel by preaching it to the heathen."

John Wesley's ministry as a missionary in America resulted in no conversions. In addition to not getting others converted under his preaching in America, he had not saved his own soul by going as a missionary. On his return trip from Savannah, while on ship, he wrote in his journal: "I went to America to convert the Indian; but oh! who shall convert me? Who is he that will deliver me from this evil heart of unbelief?"

Wesley Meets Peter Bohler

Shortly after Wesley reached England on February the 1st, 1731, he met the young Moravian, Peter Bohler. Peter Bohler soon discovered that John Wesley was groping in the dark and without the spiritual life which he needed. When Mr. Wesley said he hoped to be saved by faith and works, Peter Bohler exclaimed, "My brother, my brother, that philosophy of yours must be purged away." One of the outstanding things which Peter Bohler brought to bear to convince John Wesley of his error that he could be saved by works, was the use of the Scriptures and Christian testimony. These are spiritual forces that work mighty things for the advancement of the kingdom of God. No great revival has come apart from the Holy Scriptures, the inspired Word of God. We are hearing much talk

WESLEY'S HEART-WARMING RELIGION 9

today about a revival, the need of it, and when it may come. One thing that will accompany the revival when it does come is renewed emphasis upon the Word of God and upon Christian testimony.

John Wesley began to study the New Testament anew to find out how men were saved. He discovered that Peter Bohler was correct in his contention that we are saved by faith alone. Along with the Scriptures, Christian testimony played a prominent part in bringing John Wesley to his Aldersgate experience. Peter Bohler produced three men, all of whom testified of their own personal experience, that a true and living faith in Christ is inseparable from the sense of pardon of all past and freedom from all present sin. On hearing these testimonies, Mr. Wesley said: "I was clearly convinced of unbelief."

One of the chief heritages of Methodism is the testimony meeting. It is a sad day for the church when she abandons the testimony meeting. There has never been a revival of religion without Christian testimony. It is by such testimony that the gospel spreads from heart to heart.

Dr. A. B. Simpson, founder of the Missionary Alliance, frequently told of a scholarly minister who once gave a course of lectures on: "The Evidences of Christianity," for the special purpose of convincing and converting a wealthy and influential sceptic in his congregation. The gentleman attended his lectures and was converted. A few days later the minister ventured to ask him which of the lectures it was that impressed him decisively.

"The lectures!" answered the gentleman, "my dear

sir, I do not even remember the subject of your lectures, so I cannot say that they had any decisive influence upon my mind. I was converted by the testimony of a dear old colored woman who attended these services. As she hobbled up those steps close to me with her glad face as bright as heaven, she used to say, 'My blessed Jesus! My blessed Jesus!' and turning to me would ask, 'Do you love my blessed Jesus?' That, sir, is my evidence of Christianity."

After John Wesley heard these testimonies he said: "I was clearly convinced of unbelief." When he resolved to quit preaching because he deemed it inconsistent to preach to others the faith he did not possess himself, Peter Bohler gave him the following advice: "No, you are not to cease preaching; preach faith until you have it, then because you have it you will preach faith."

John Wesley heeded the advice of Peter Bohler, found the heart warming experience, and began immediately to preach in the pulpit that salvation comes through faith alone. The response to such preaching was to have church doors closed in his face. In ten pulpits where he preached within a short period of time, six of the churches informed him: "Sir, you must preach here no more."

Another shock came to Wesley when Peter Bohler informed him that we are not only saved by faith, but that salvation is an instantaneous work of grace. This Mr. Wesley could not believe, and again he fell back upon the Scriptures and Christian testimony for verification of Bohler's contention. On searching the Scripture Wesley discovered in the New Testament, to use his own words: "Scarce any instances are there other than instantaneous conversion." Peter Bohler again produced a number of witnesses to testify that their conversions were instantaneous. On hearing these testimonies Mr. Wesley said: "Herein is my dispute, I could only cry out, 'Lord, help thou mine unbelief'."

On the day before John Wesley's conversion at Aldersgate, May 24, 1738, he wrote to a friend, and in this letter he declared that he was "full of abominable sin, and under the curse and the wrath of God."

The Heart Warming Testimony

Following his earnest search of the Scriptures and the hearing of testimonies concerning instantaneous conversion by faith, John Wesley came to Aldersgate, where he too was instantly transformed through a saving faith in Christ. Mr. Wesley now became a witness to the saving grace of God in his heart. He wrote in his journal: "I then testified openly to all there present what I now first felt in my heart."

On the same night, following John Wesley's Aldersgate experience, there was an after-meeting in an upstairs room on a nearby street called Little Britain. Charles Wesley, the brother of John, was at the time in that room sick with the palsy. It was to this room that John Wesley resorted with a few friends. On the previous day Charles Wesley had undergone a similar experience to that of John at Aldersgate Street. Charles Wesley had written a hymn on the occasion of his conversion, which was the first hymn ever written by one of the greatest hymn writers of all time.

12 WESLEY'S HEART-WARMING RELIGION

It was about ten o'clock when John Wesley with a group of friends entered the room of Charles, and rushing to his bedside cried out to his brother: "I believe!" The two brothers rejoiced together with a few of their friends in their new found experience. That night that whole company united in singing the hymn which Charles Wesley had written on the previous day. It was the first Methodist hymn ever written, and the first Methodist hymn ever sung. A stanza of the hymn is as follows:

> "Where shall my wandering soul begin?
> How shall I pause to heaven aspire?
> A slave redeemed from death and sin
> A brand plucked from eternal fire.
> How shall I equal triumphs raise,
> Or sing my great Deliverer's praise?"

When he awoke the next morning he said: "In my heart and on my lips were the words, 'Jesus, Master.'"

The great transformation that came to John Wesley in obtaining the strangely warmed heart is well illustrated in the answers John gave to his father when he was urged to leave Oxford and assume the pastorate at Epworth. John refused to go, and some of the reasons he set forth for not going were, that at the university, he had delightful daily converse with his friends, retirement, freedom from care, a regular income paid on time, servants ready at hand. At Epworth he could not tolerate the food; the work would interfere with his sleeping habits; there were too many people to be looked after, and the people were very rude and ungrateful. But after Aldersgate such excuses as he offered about going to Epworth were swept completely out of his life.

It was the experience of Aldersgate that made John Wesley the "prophet of the long road," and caused him for fifty years to ride on an average of 5,000 miles a year, and preach during that time on an average of nearly three times a day. It was the experience of Aldersgate that gave him the incentive to write 230 books and pamphlets, and to build schools and chapels by the scores and hundreds. It was that experience that caused him to enter with an abandonment and enthusiasm into all the political and social movements of his day.

On Sanctification

Much discussion has centered about the doctrine of entire sanctification as interpreted and proclaimed by John Wesley. The doctrine of sanctification was not a side issue in the preaching and teaching of Mr. Wesley. It was a major thesis. It was a matter of great insistency and urgency with him.

According to Mr. Wesley, sanctification was obtainable in this life, in contrast to the widely accepted doctrine that sanctification is obtainable only in the hour of death. It is not possible to understand the genius of the Wesleyan revival without coming to grips with Wesley's doctrine of sanctification.

The major emphasis which Wesley placed upon the possibility of securing complete victory over sin in this life, was a tap root of the great spiritual awakening which began under his preaching and those associated with him.

Mr. Wesley held that sanctification is both a process and an instantaneous epoch following justification. In his sermon "Working Out Our Own Salvation," he says: "By justification we are saved from the guilt of sin, and restored to the favor of God; by sanctification we are saved from the power and root of sin, and restored to the image of God. All experience, as well as Scripture, show this salvation to be both instantaneous and gradual. It begins the moment we are justified, in the holy, humble, gentle, patient love of God and man. It gradually increases from that moment, as 'a grain of mustard seed, which at first, is the least of all seeds,' but afterwards puts forth large branches and becomes a great tree; till in another instant, the heart is cleansed from all sin, and filled with the pure love of God and man. Even that love increases more and more, till we 'grow up in all things into him that is our head;' till we 'attain the measure of the stature of the fulness of Christ.'"

A Distinguished Theologian On Wesley's Views

We have a number of eminent writers who have sought to make it appear that John Wesley was not clear in his own thinking on the subject of sanctification. Some of these writers claim that Mr. Wesley held varying views of sanctification and they seek to leave a cloud of uncertainty over the Wesleyan doctrine of sanctification. One of the most eminent and influential writers in this field, in wielding a wide infleunce in Methodist circles, was Dr. Wilbur F. Tillett, who for many years was dean of the School of Theology at Vanderbilt University. He was the author of "Studies in Christian Doctrine, Pertaining to the Spiritual Life." This book was widely used as a text for Methodist preachers and was in the course of study for many years.

Dr. Tillett differs from a number of the other great Methodist theologians in his interpretation of John Wesley's view of sanctification. Dr. Tillett held the view that that element of the sinful nature, spoken of as "the root of sin," or "inbred sin," which many believe is removed in an epochal experience subsequent to regeneration, is removed at the time of regeneration.

Dr. Tillett taught that Mr. Wesley held two views upon the subject of sanctification. Concerning the first view of Mr. Wesley, Dr. Tillett says: "The first view is that which regards every child of God who measures up to the ideal state of a justified and regenerate believer, as 'perfect' in a New Testament sense of that term."

Concerning the second view he says: "The second view of Christian perfection identifies it with sanctification, and is based on the idea that to be a truly justified and regenerate child of God, is not in itself alone to possess Christian perfection." The paragraph under which this second view is discussed bears the heading: "Entire Sanctification an instantaneous experience subsequent to regeneration."

In the conclusion of his book Dr. Tillett has a paragraph bearing the title; "A Possible Basis of Agreement." In this paragraph he says: "Recognizing two distinct theories of entire sanctification as involved

16 WESLEY'S HEART-WARMING RELIGION

in his writings, let us stress the point which he admitted as possible that—'instantaneous sanctification,' though generally occurring later, may take place at conversion—and we will thereby obliterate all necessary and radical difference between his two theories."

It is significant that even Dr. Tillett admits the predominant view of John Wesley's was "instantaneous sanctification" subsequent to regeneration.

While Dr. Tillett urges salvation from both the guilt of sin and the being of sin at conversion, he makes this rather interesting statement: "If it be found that any one who thinks he has been converted comes to the consciousness of sin in himself of any kind—'inbred sin', sins of temper, pride, self will, etc.—let us insist that he needs, and must have at once, a further radical and instantaneous work of grace in order to be saved from all sin; and let that work be called by any Scripture name that may suggest itself to any one as most proper."

It is very interesting indeed to read such a statement after wading through the major thesis of Dr. Tillett to the effect that sanctification is obtained at conversion. If we follow his instruction relative to urging believers who have the consciousness of "inbred sin", sins of temper, pride, self will, etc., to seek an instantaneous work of grace subsequent to regeneration, how many believers would be fit subjects for such exhortation?

Again we bring forward the verdict of Christian experience across the pathway of centuries. Let that experience be heeded by the church in the light of Dr. Tillett's exhortation, and we will begin the proclamation of a definite Pentecost for believers from every pulpit in the land. One thing is very clear in Dr. Tillett's discussion. While contending for sanctification at conversion, he admits the possibility of conversion without sanctification; and that sanctification may come as a work subsequent to regeneration, as an instantaneous work of grace through faith, which saves from all sin.

Any varying views which theologians may have discovered in Mr. Wesley's writings upon the subject of sanctification, should not be taken as arguments to cast a cloud or a question mark over his main thesis on sanctification as an instantaneous work, subsequent to regeneration, whereby the heart is delivered from all sin.

Any varying views that have been discovered would indicate that Mr. Wesley had thoroughly weighed the evidence that brought him to his culminating and predominant view of sanctification as a work of grace subsequent to regeneration. There were processes of growth in Mr. Wesley's thinking which brought him to his final and ultimate view of sanctification as a work of grace subsequent to regeneration.

Two Epochs In Christian Experience

The emphasis which is found in Wesley's sermons and writings on justification by faith and sanctification by faith, as two distinct works of grace is clear and unmistakable.

In his sermon on the new birth, Mr. Wesley says: "The new birth is not the same with sanctification." (Page 45, Vol. I, Wesley's Works.)

18 WESLEY'S HEART-WARMING RELIGION

Mr. Wesley was surprised when he discovered that entire sanctification is an experience which may be obtained instantaneously by believers subsequent to regeneration. In his sermon on Patience, Mr. Wesley says: "Four, five and forty years ago, when I had no distinct views of what the apostle meant, by exhorting us to 'leave the principles of the doctrine of Christ, and go on to perfection;' two or three persons in London, whom I knew to be truly sincere, desired to give me an account of their experience. It appeared exceeding strange, being different from any that I had heard before: but exactly similar to the preceding account of entire sanctification." (P. 223, Vol. II, Wesley's Works).

Mr. Wesley did not accept the doctrine of entire sanctification as a second definite work of grace without cautious investigation. In the same sermon, he speaks of his cautious investigation: "A few years after I desired all those in London, who made the same profession, to come to me altogether in the foundry, that I might be thoroughly satisfied, I desired that man of God, Thomas Walsh, to give us the meeting there. When we met, first one of us, then the other, asked then the most searching questions we could devise.

"They answered every one without hesitation and with the utmost simplicity, so that we were fully persuaded that they did not deceive themselves. In the years 1759, 1760, 1761, and 1762, their numbers multiplied exceedingly, not only in London and Bristol, but in various parts of Ireland as well as England. Not trusting to the testimony of others, I carefully examined most of these myself; and in London alone, I found 652 members of our society, who were exceeding clear in their experience, and whose testimony I could see no reason to doubt."

In the course of his investigation Mr. Wesley discovered that in no case was sanctification wrought gradually, but that in every case it came an instantaneous work of grace in response to faith in Christ, not only as Saviour, but also as sanctifier. Concerning this discovery, he speaks in the same sermon: "I believe no years have passed, since that time, wherein God has not wrought the same work in many others, but sometimes in one part of England or Ireland, sometimes in another;—as 'the wind bloweth where it listeth;' and every one of these (after the most careful inquiry) I have not found one exception either in Britain or Ireland (has declared his deliverance from sin was instantaneous); that the change was wrought in a moment.

"Had the half of these, or one-third, or one and twenty, declared it was gradually wrought in them, I should have believed this, in regard to them, and thought that some were gradually sanctified and some instantaneously, but as I have not found, in so long a space of time, a single person speaking thus; as all who believe they are sanctified, declare with one voice, that the change was wrought in a moment. I cannot but believe, that sanctification is commonly, if not always, an instantaneous work."

Mixed Holiness

Mr. Wesley described the holiness in the heart of the Christian preceding his entire sanctification as a mixed holiness. He speaks of this mixed holiness in the same sermon, on "Patience". He says: "Until this, universal change was wrought in his soul, all his holiness was mixed, he was humble, but not entirely; his humility was mixed with pride: he was meek, but his meekness was frequently interrupted by anger, or some uneasy and turbulent passion.

"His love was frequently dampened by the love of some creature; the love of his neighbor, by evil surmising, or some thought, if not temper, contrary to love. His will was not wholly melted down into the will of God; but altho in general he could say, 'I come not to do my own will, but the will of him that sent me'; yet now and then nature rebelled, and could not clearly say, 'Lord, not as I will but as thou wilt'." (P. 222, Vol. II, Wesley's Works).

Immediately following his description of the mixed holiness of the believer preceding his sanctification, he describes the state of the believer following his sanctification: "His whole soul is now consistent with itself; there is no jarring strain. All his passions flow in a continual stream, with an even tenor, to God. To him, that has entered into his rest, you may truly say,

> 'Come thou every art within,
> All ruffled, all serene!'

"There is no mixture of any contrary affection; all is peace and harmony after. Being filled with love, there is no more interruption of it, than of the beating of his heart; and continual love bringing continual joy in the Lord, he rejoices evermore. He converses continually with God whom he loves, unto whom in everything he gives thanks. And as he now loves God with all his heart, and with all his soul, and with all his mind, and with all his strength; the Lord Jesus now reigns alone in his heart, the Lord of every motion there."

The message of holiness, as a definite experience obtainable subsequent to regeneration, was a dominant note of emphasis in the Wesleyan revival. The dominant note of emphasis in the protestant reformation under the leadership of Martin Luther, was justification by faith. Large emphasis was given in the Wesleyan revival to the doctrine of justification by faith and the witness of the Spirit. But the crowning emphasis in the Wesleyan revival was on the doctrine of sanctification as a definite experience for believers, obtainable by faith in this life.

Justification and Sanctification

Mr. Wesley preached a sermon on the subject, "God's Vineyard," using as a text the Scripture found in Isaiah 5:4: "What could have been done more to my vineyard, but I have not done it? Wherefore, when I looked that it should bring forth grapes, brought it forth wild grapes?" He applied the text in its narrower sense to "the body of people commonly called Methodists." He treats the text under four heads, in regard to doctrine, scriptural helps, discipline and outward protection. The sermon clearly reveals that the

22 WESLEY'S HEART-WARMING RELIGION

crowning doctrinal emphasis of the Wesleyan revival was sanctification.

The sermon points out the able emphasis on the doctrine of justification by faith, in the protestant reformation, under the leadership of Martin Luther, and also calls attention to Luther's inadequate understanding of sanctification. He says: "Who has written more ably than Martin Luther, on justification by faith alone? And who was more ignorant of the doctrine of sanctification, or more confused in his conceptions of it? In order to be thoroughly convinced of this, of his total ignorance with regard to sanctification, there needs no more than to read over, without prejudice, his celebrated comment on the Epistle to the Galatians." (P. 389, Wesley's Works, Vol. II).

Following his discussion of Luther's inadequate knowledge of sanctification, Mr. Wesley says: "For it has pleased God to give the Methodists a full and clear knowledge of each, and the wide difference between them. They know, indeed, that at the same time a man is justified, sanctification properly begins, for when he is justified, he is 'born again', 'born from above', 'born of the Spirit'; which altho it is not (as some suppose) the whole process of sanctification, is doubtless the gate of it."

Mr. Wesley speaks of regeneration as the gate of entry to the path which leads to sanctification. He speaks of regeneration as the gate of entry in strong and forceful words. He says: "Of this, likewise, God has given them a full view. They know, the new birth implies a great change in the soul, in him that is 'born of the Spirit', as was wrought in his body when

he was born of a woman: not an outward change only
. . . but an inward change for all unholy, to all holy
tempers; from pride, to humility; from passionateness to meekness; from peevishness and discontent,
to patience and resignation; in a word, from an earthly,
sensual, devilish mind, to a mind that was in Christ
Jesus."

Immediately following this strong word on regeneration, Mr. Wesley affirmed that regeneration was
not sanctification. He says: "No; it is only the threshold of sanctification; the first entrance upon it . . .
the new birth, therefore, is the first point of sanctification, which may increase more and more unto the
perfect day."

Early Methodists and the Warmhearted Experience

Mr. Wesley expressed great gratitude for the fact
that the Methodists laid equal stress on justification
and sanctification. He says: "It is, then, a great
blessing given to the people that as they do not think
or speak of Justification so as to supersede sanctification; so neither do they think or speak of sanctification,
so as to supersede justification. They take care to
keep each in his own place! lay equal stress on one
and the other.

"They know, God has joined these together, and it
is not for man to put them asunder; therefore they
maintain, with equal zeal and diligence, the doctrine
of free, full and present justification, on one hand; and
of entire sanctification both of heart and life, on the
others; being as tenacious of inward holiness, as any

mystic; and of outward, as any Pharisee." (P. 390, Wesley's Works, Vol. II).

Describing the early rise of Methodism Mr. Wesley said: "Two young clergymen, not very remarkable in any way, of middle age, having a tolerable measure of health, tho rather weak than strong, began, about fifteen years ago, to call sinners to repentance. This they did, for a time, in many of the churches in and about London, but two difficulties arose; First, the churches were so crowded, that many of the parishioners could not get in; secondly, they preached new doctrines; that we are saved by faith, and that 'without holiness, no man can see the Lord.' For one or other of these reasons, they were not long-suffered to preach in the churches. They then preached in Moorfields, Kennington, Common, and many other public places.

"The fruit of their preaching quickly appeared. Many sinners were changed both in heart and life, but it seemed, this could not continue long, for every one clearly saw, these preachers would quickly wear themselves out; and no clergyman dare to assist them. But soon one and another, tho not ordained, offered to assist them. God gave a signal blessing to their word. Many sinners were thoroly convinced of sin, and many truly converted to God. Their assistance increased, both in number and in the success of their labors. Some of them were learned; some unlearned; most of them were young; a few middle aged: some of them were weak, some, on the contrary, of remarkably strong understanding. But it pleased God to own them all; so that more and more brands were plucked out of the burning." (P. 391, Wesley's Works, Vol. II).

Justification and Sanctification By Faith

In his sermon on the Scriptural way of salvation, Mr. Wesley proclaims with great emphasis that both justification and sanctification come by definite acts of faith. He says: " 'But do you believe we are sanctified by faith? We know you believe that we are justified by faith; but do you believe, and accordingly teach, that we are sanctified by our works? So it has been roundly and vehemently affirmed for these five and twenty years: but I have constantly declared that just the contrary; and that in all manner of ways. I have continually testified in private and in public, that we are sanctified as well as justified by faith. And indeed the one of those great truths does not exceedingly illustrate the other. Exactly as we are justified by faith, so we are sanctified by faith. Faith is the condition, and the only condition of sanctification, exactly as it is of justification. It is the condition: none is sanctified, but he that believes; without faith no man is sanctified. And it is the only condition: this alone is sufficient for sanctification. Every one that believes is sanctified, whatever else he has or has not. In other words, no man is sanctified till he believes: Every man when he believes is sanctified." (P. 388, Wesley's Works, Vol. I).

In the same sermon Mr. Wesley condemns with strong and vigorous words the doctrine that the heart is cleansed from all sin in the moment of justification. He says: "Hence may appear the extreme mischievousness of that seemingly interested opinion, that there is no sin in a believer; that all sin is destroyed, root and branch, the moment a man is justified. By totally preventing that repentance, it quite blocks up the way to sanctification: there is no place for repentance in him who believes that there is no sin either in his life or heart: consequently there is no place for his being perfected in love, to which that repentance is indispensably necessary. (P. 390, Wesley's Works, Vol. I).

"Hence it may likewise appear, that there is no possible danger in thus expecting full salvation. For suppose we were mistaken, suppose no such blessing ever was or can be attained, yet we lose nothing: nay, that every expectation quickens in using all the talents which God has given us; yea, in improving them all: so that when our Lord cometh, He will receive his own with increase." (P. 390, Wesley's Works, Vol. I).

Without Faith Nothing Avails For The Warmhearted Experience

John Wesley proclaimed faith to be "the essential condition for sanctification." We quote further from his sermon, "Scriptural Way of Salvation": "But to return. Tho it be allowed, that both this repentance and its fruits are necessary to full salvation; yet they are not necessary either in the same sense with faith, or in the same degree: not in the same degree—but these fruits are necessary conditionally, if there be time and opportunity for them; otherwise a man may be sanctified without them. But he cannot be sanctified without faith. Likewise, let a man have ever so much of this repentance, or ever so many good works, yet all this does not at all avail: he is not sanctified till he believes: but the moment he believes, with or without those fruits, yea with more or less of this repentance, he is sanctified—not in the same sense;—for this repentance and these fruits are only remotely necessary, necessary in order to the continuance of his faith, as well the increase of it; whereas faith is immediately and directly necessary to sanctification. It remains, that faith is the only condition, which is immediately and approximately necessary to sanctification.

"But what is that faith whereby we are sanctified? Saved from sin and perfected in love? 'It is divine evidence and conviction, first, that God hath promised it in the Holy Scriptures. Till we are thoroly satisfied of this, there is no moving one step farther. And one would imagine there needed not one word more to satisfy reasonable man of this and the ancient promise, 'then will I circumcise thy heart and the heart of thy seed, to love the Lord thy God with all thy heart, and with all thy soul, and with all thy mind'. How clearly does this express the being perfected in love! How strongly imply the being saved from all sin! For as long as love takes up the whole heart, what room is there for sin therein?'

"It is a divine evidence and conviction, secondly, what God hath promised he is able to perform. Admitting, therefore, that 'with men it is impossible' to 'bring a clean thing out of an unclean', to purify the heart from all sin, and to fill it with all holiness: yet this creates no difficulty in the case, seeing 'with

God all things are possible.' And surely no one ever imagined it was possible to any power less than that of the Almighty! But if God speaks, it shall be done. God saith, 'Let there be light; and there (is) light'.

"It is, thirdly, a divine evidence and conviction that he is able and willing to do it now. And why not? Is not a moment to him the same as a thousand years? He cannot want more time to accomplish whatever is his will. And he cannot want or stay for any more worthiness or fitness in the persons he is pleased to honor. We may therefore boldly say, at any point of time, 'now is the day of salvation!' 'Today, if ye will hear his voice, harden not your hearts!' 'Behold, all things are now ready, come unto the marriage!'

"To this confidence, that God is both able and willing to sanctify us now, there needs to be added one thing more, a divine evidence and conviction that he doeth it. In that hour it is done: God says to the inmost soul, 'According to thy faith be it unto thee!' Then the soul is pure from every spot of sin; it is clean 'from all unrighteousness.' The believer then experiences the deep meaning of those solemn words, 'If we walk in the light as he is in the light, we have fellowship one with another, and the blood of Jesus Christ his Son cleanseth us from all sin'." (pp. 390, 391, Vol. I, Wesley's Works).

When May the Christian Be Sanctified?

Sanctification was a subject that was up for frequent discussion by John Wesley and his co-laborers. The questions and answers in one of these discussions pertain to the time when we may be sanctified. The question was raised: "When does inward sanctification begin?" Answer: In the moment we are justified. The seed of every virtue is then sown in the soul. At that time the believer gradually dies to sin, and grows in grace. Yet sin remains in him: Yea, the seed of all sin, till he is sanctified throughout in spirit, soul and body."

The question was asked: "Is it ordinarily given till a little before death?" Answer: "It is not, to those who expect it no sooner, nor consequently ask for it, at least, not in faith." Question: "But ought we to expect it sooner?" Answer: "Why not?" Question: "But would not one who was thus sanctified be capable of worldly business?" Answer: "He would be far more capable of it than ever, as going through all without distraction." Question: "Would he be capable of marriage?" Answer: "Why should he not?"

Still further questions are raised in the discussion. Question: "In what manner should we preach entire sanctification?" Answer: "Scarce at all to those who are not pressing forward. To those who are, always by way of promise; always drawing, rather than driving." Question: "How would we wait for the fulfilling of the promise?" Answer: "In universal obedience; in keeping all the commandments; in denying ourselves and taking up our cross daily. These are the general means which God has ordained for our receiving the sanctifying grace. The particular are, prayer, searching the Scriptures, communicating, and fasting." (pp. 201, 202, Vol. V, Wesley's Works).

We have abundant testimony from eminent theologians that the culminating prevailing doctrine of John Wesley on sanctification held that sanctification is an instantaneous work of grace coming by faith subsequent to regeneration. Among these eminent theologians is Dr. Olin Alfred Curtis whose work on systematic theology has been used as a text in a number of Methodist seminaries and has also been included in courses of study for Methodist preachers. Dr. Curtis was for many years professor of systematic theology in Drew Theological Seminary. Dr. Curtis is very clear in his statements concerning the teaching of John Wesley on the subject of sanctification. In giving his interpretation of John Wesley's teaching, he says: "According to John Wesley, a sinner has three things the matter with him: First, he is guilty; second, he is morally powerless; and, third, his inherent and inherited disposition is wrong. Or, as I would say, the individuality is out of harmony with the ideal of the moral person. When a sinner is justified the guilt is cancelled. When he is regenerated he receives a nucleus of power, not enough 'to exterminate his wrong disposition, but enough to fight it to a standstill.' In Christian perfection, there is no such fight with the disposition, 'no civil war at all' for the wrong impulse never enters the consciousness as motive." (The Christian Faith, Curtis, P. 382-383).

Another Noted Theologian Interprets Wesley's Views

Dr. Olin Curtis gives a concrete illustration to illustrate the meaning and significance of holiness as taught by John Wesley. In presenting the illustration he says: "It will help us all probably, if I give a concrete illustration of Wesley's view. Here is a man, a Christian preacher, now who has from infancy been naturally jealous. He is not only converted, but as a noble Christian man, ready to sacrifice for his Lord, and equally ready to serve his brethren. But he is still jealous in disposition. Yesterday he heard another preacher's sermon receive large commendation and like an uprush of mercury in the heat, that old feeling of jealousy rose into consciousness. His volition, his personality, had no more to do with it than his will had to do with the coming on of night. But the moment our preacher realizes that he is jealous he makes Christian battle, and forces the disposition back, back into its cave. Now, we have here an exceedingly strange psychological situation, for the man's struggle is plainly Christian in its revelation of the moral ideal, and yet the struggle reveals a motive life which no Christian ought to have at all. Or, we can say this: the victory is truly that of a Christian man—but as a Christian man he should have been without the possibility of that kind of a battle. Now comes a pivotal inquiry. As our preacher grows what does his growth in grace accomplish? According to Wesley, the growth does not affect the inherent disposition of jealousy at all; but it does bring the regenerate man himself to a more potent attitude, both of intolerance toward the disposition and of trust toward Jesus Christ. With this more potent personal attitude the man dares to believe that his Lord can and will take that jealousy, and every wrong disposition out of his life. In full, simple faith he asks Christ to do it; and precisely as when he was unconverted, it is all done at one stroke. Now what is the man's condition? On the one hand, he never is conscious of jealousy. Rather does he spontaneously rejoice in another man's success. On the other hand, he never comes to self-consciousness without being filled, like the prodigality of a freshet, with the love of God. This, as I understand him, is what John Wesley means for the conquest of inbred sin thru supreme love. If there is one man here to whom Wesley's view of inbred sin suggests no reality, no point in kindred experience, he most surely is to be regarded as extremely fortunate." (The Christian Faith—Curtis—pp. 383-384).

The Test of Scriptural Argument And Modern Scholarship

After giving this analysis of John Wesley's view of Christian perfection, Dr. Curtis raises the question as to whether or not Mr. Wesley's view will stand the test of scriptural argument, in the light of modern scholarship. Speaking on this point, Dr. Curtis says: "Is there, tho, for this Wesleyan doctrine of Christian perfection any support in Biblical theology? In Wesley's day there was such an arbitrary and fragmentary and superficial use of Scriptures, even by the finest scholars, that many students have gained the impression of, if not the belief, that the Scriptural argument for Christian perfection cannot endure the test of our modern method of studying the Bible. I am certain that the test can be endured." After making this statement, Dr. Curtis gives several pages to presenting the scriptural grounds for Christian perfection.

Dr. Curtis believes that Christian perfection also has a sound psychological basis. In speaking of the psychological basis of Christian perfection, he says: "As we have seen, the motive life of a regenerate man is organized about the motive of loyalty to Christ. The motive of loyalty is not a simple motive, but is made up of two elements, one of love and the other of duty. At rare moments these two elements are in self-consciousness with equal force, but usually the sense of duty is paramount. The regenerate man, in any typical situation, is seeking to do his duty. His common remark is: 'I will be true! I will not deny my Lord.' This loyalty is very different from the loyalty of the moralist; and for two reasons, namely, it is loyalty to a person, and it is rooted in the enthusiasm of a positive personal affection. And yet the Christian loyalty has some of the same psychological weakness which renders morality so ineffective. Duty always implies a conflict, a civil war. The sense of the ought is, like a bugle, intended to call the person into battle. And while this moral battle is great, it is less than the highest mood. You will see what I mean, if you think of a home where husband, wife, parents, children are ever trying to do their duty to each other. What a dreadful home that would be! Not one day with the simple, rejoicing impulse of dominant love.

"In personal holiness this motive of loyalty is transformed into the simple motive of pure love. There remains all of the ethical quality of duty, for the new supreme love is a moral love; but 'the whip of the ought' is gone. The holy person does not do things because it is his duty to do them, but because he loves to do them. But note this closely, the important thing here, psychologically, is not the vastness of the love (that is a matter of endless growth) but simply that the love entirely occupies the self-conscious mood. Whenever the persons comes to self-consciousness it it crammed with love to the very edges. Thus, there is a perfect personal organism, because all of the man's motivity is nothing but love in a variety of shapes. In the man's personal life there is no antagonism, no civil war whatever. He may be tempted, as we shall see, but he cannot be tempted by his own inorganic condition, by his own depravity."

The Ultimate Stroke

Dr. Curtis lays emphasis upon the crisis by which the regenerate enter into the experience of Christian perfection. He recognizes, of course, a growth preceding the crisis and a growth following it. He says: "But is personal holiness obtained gradually by earnest endeavor? Looking at it in the most comprehensive way, our answer should be in the affirmative; for the crisis itself is profoundly involved in all that has led up to it."

Following this statement concerning the growth preceding the crisis, Dr. Curtis magnifies Wesley's emphasis upon the ultimate stroke. Concerning the importance of this "ultimate stroke," he says: "And yet John Wesley's emphasis upon the ultimate stroke is exceedingly important. For there is a great difference between the last phase of the regenerate life

WESLEY'S HEART-WARMING RELIGION 35

and the first phase of the life of supreme love. As it is only in the latter case that the motive of loyalty entirely loses the note of duty; only in the latter case that love absolutely fills self-consciousness to its rim; so only in the latter case that all the wrong motives of disposition are exhausted.

"But the question has been asked, 'Why, on the principle of your discussion of motivity, may a regenerate man, with his motive of loyalty, not fight his way into personal holiness?' My answer is this: To exhaust all wrong motive by a sheer negative fight would require more time than belongs to our earthly life; and even if there were time enough the victory would exalt the element of duty and not the element of love in the motive of loyalty. What we are after is so to escape sin as to escape the bondage of conscience itself, and like God himself, live the life of moral love." (The Christian Faith—Curtis. P. 391-392).

John Wesley won for himself world wide recognition as an authority on holiness. Dr. Curtis, in his work on systematic theology already referred to, says: "Historically, Wesley had almost the same epochal relation to the doctrinal emphasis upon holiness that Luther had to the doctrinal emphasis upon justification by faith, or that Athenasius had to the doctrinal emphasis upon the Deity of our Lord." (Christian Faith —Curtis. P. 373). Curtis believes that Wesley was a much more reliable authority on the subject of holiness than many modern teachers who try to discount his teaching on the subject. As the leader of an epochal movement Curtis says that Wesley "had at hand quantity in data." In adding further comment,

Curtis says: "The flaw in some of the modern discussions of Christian perfection is not so much in the reasoning as in the want of sufficient data to reason upon." No man of modern times has had a greater "quantity in data" to draw from than John Wesley, and few if any have had such a quantity.

John Wesley not only possessed "quantity in data", but he also possessed a "surety and discrimination". In making this observation Curtis says: "There are several recent scientific studies on Christian experience which would be almost priceless in value had the authors only known the difference between reality and imitation. It is possible to obtain a thousand answers to a list of questions, and have only one hundred of them with any real Christian meaning. It was just at this point that John Wesley was a master in Israel . . . Wesley had such extraordinary spiritual insight, and such sanity of judgment, that often his most casual statement, especially in his journal, is more illuminating than any profound monographs in theology." (Christian Faith—Curtis. P. 374).

A Noted Theologian Answers Obections

This doctrine of sanctification for the heart of the believer, which was so prominent in the teaching and preaching of the early Methodists, has become "the missing link" in wide circles of present day Methodism.

Perhaps many of our preachers and teachers have come to believe that such men as John Wesley, Adam Clarke, John Fletcher, and Francis Asbury, were mistaken in their interpretations of this great experience.

WESLEY'S HEART-WARMING RELIGION 37

It is quite interesting to note how some modern writers sidestep the issue with explanations and interpretations, which really rob the Wesleyan doctrine of sanctification of its vitality, so far as its practical realization is concerned in our modern day church life.

Some, no doubt, labor under the opinion that the Wesleyan doctrine of sanctification is contradicted by the acid test of modern philosophy. There are still others who feel that the doctrine meets insuperable obstacles in the human body, and still others feel that it is contrary to revelation found in God's Word.

The late Henry C. Sheldon, for many years a professor in Boston University, is author of "System of Christian Doctrine" which has been used as a text in theological seminaries, and in the course of study for Methodist preachers. Dr. Sheldon, who has been regarded as a profound thinker in high scholastic circles, is of the opinion that the objections commonly raised to the doctrine of sanctification for believers are not valid.

In speaking of the objections commonly raised to the experience of sanctification for the believer, Dr. Sheldon says: "Can this goal be reached in the present life? In other words, can a man advance here to a state which may be described negatively as free from sin, and positively as under the complete dominion of love—a state in which the moral disposition is pure and normal through and through, and conduct fails to be ideal in all respects only thru unavoidable creatively limitations? It must be granted that observation teaches us that the period of earthly discipline is in general all too short to consummate in this sense the work of sanctification. But, on the other hand, where is the warrant for assuming that such consummation is strictly impossible? Philosophy certainly does not afford it, that is, a philosophy that is consummate with Christian principles. It cannot be said that the body is an insuperable obstacle to entire sanctification, for Christian truth does not allow that there is any essential sense in matter. If there is, then, any insuperable obstacle, it must be in the spirit. The human spirit is indeed finite, fallible and infirm; but now one of these qualities stands in necessary opposition to holiness. As for the sinful bias by which it is affected, who can say on grounds of reason that it is beyond remedy within the limits of earthly life? Great moral transformations are wrought in very brief intervals of time.

"Who then, is authorized to affirm that it is beyond the comprehension of God's remedial agency to completely sanctify a soul before death?" (System of Christian Doctrine—Sheldon. P. 464).

Obtainable In This Life

Dr. Sheldon gives scriptural argument for obtaining sanctification in this life. He says:

"A rational warrant for denying the possibility of entire sanctification in this life being thus wanting, the ground of denial must be found, if discovered at all, in revelation. It must be proved that the Scriptures teach that it is outside of the divine ability or the divine purpose to consummate the sanctification of any subject of grace before the article of death. Calvinists are hindered, of course, by their postulate from assuming that it is beyond the divine ability to do this, and non-Calvinists must need to spare of sustaining this assumption from the Scripture. In the face of such words as those of Paul, which describe God as 'able to do exceeding abundantly above all that we ask or think.' It remains then to deduce from the Scriptures that it is outside the divine purpose or no part of the divine economy to bring any one to the point of entire sanctification in this life. But who has ever made a deduction of this sort which has even the appearance of legitimacy? Various passages show, indeed, that every man has unmistakable occasion to include himself in the ranks of sinners when his life is taken as a whole. Not one of these, however, gives the faintest indication that its author meant to teach that in no case can sin be entirely put away before the separation of soul and body. Take for example, this declaration of John: 'If we say we have no sin, we deceive ourselves, and the truth is not in us.' What an eccentricity of exegesis to suppose that this teaching is a necessary continuance in sin, when the next verse read, 'If we confess our sins, he is faithful and just to forgive us our sins, and to cleanse us from all unrighteousness.' " (System of Christian Doctrine—Sheldon. P. 465).

Dr. Sheldon closes his discussion of the possibility of sanctification for the believer in this life with these interesting words:

"The New Testament gives no grounds for supposing that there is such an absolute contrast between the conditions of the heavenly life and those of Christian life in this world that sin must be entirely alien to the one and inevitable to the other. In the absence of such a contrast, the command, instructions, and prayers which look to entire sanctification or perfect love, carry a certain presumption that the state which these terms define is a possible attainment in this life. It must be confessed, however, that it stands forth as an exceedingly high ideal. Any one who understands all that it implies will despair of its possibility, save as his heart is quickened by a large and intense faith in the marvelous power of divine grace." (System of Christian Doctrine—Sheldon. P. 468).

A Major Emphasis of Early Methodists

Umphrey Lee, Chancellor of Southern Methodist University, in his book, "John Wesley and Modern Religion", introduces chapter 8 of the book with the statement: "Wesley's most distinctive doctrine is unquestionably that of Christian perfection." He further says in the same chapter: 'Without holiness no man can see the Lord,' was Wesley's uncompromising slogan." In the same chapter Dr. Lee quotes a statement of John Wesley's made in 1767, in which he summarizes his thoughts on Christian perfection: "I believe this perfection is always wrought in the soul by a simple act of faith; consequently in an instant. But I believe a gradual work, both preceding and following that instant. As to the time—I believe this instant generally is the instant of death, the moment before the soul leaves the body; but I believe it may be ten, twenty, or forty years before. I believe it is usually many years after justification; but that it may be with-

WESLEY'S HEART-WARMING RELIGION

in five years or five months after it, I know no conclusive argument to the contrary."

Dr. Lee further says: "As to the origin and development of this doctrine of Christian perfection, Wesley had much to say. If it were possible, it would be better to reprint 'A Plain Account of Christian Perfection', which he wrote in 1765, and printed the next year."

Gilbert T. Rowe, well-known educator and theologian, in his book, "The Meaning of Methodism", quotes John Wesley as writing toward the end of his life these words: "Blessed be God, tho we set a hundred enthusiasts aside, we are still 'compassed with a cloud of witnesses,' who have testified, and do testify, in life and in death, that perfection which I have taught these forty years." Dr. Rowe in speaking of the emphasis placed by early Methodists on holiness, says:

"In the early days both sinners and Christians were invited to come to the altar, the former for conversion, and the latter for sanctification. There is now in a church in England an old Methodist register, upon which the names are marked, 'Seeker', 'Saved', 'Sanctified'. Reports of many of the early camp meetings in this country gave so many 'saved', then so many 'sanctified', and when Asbury made his last trip through the south, the burden of his message was the instantaneous experience of entire sanctification. Several of the old disciples earnestly urged the preachers to preach sanctification as an instantaneous second work of grace. And yet, while this view has persisted in groups within the large branches of Methodism, and also in smaller churches which have separated from them, it has never been able to get a hold upon the general Methodist conscience."

A Criticism of Wesley's Position

Dr. Rowe, in making further comment, says: "Why is this? Why has the experience, variously designated 'the second blessing', and 'entire sanctification,' 'the second work of grace,' 'the baptism of the Spirit,' and 'baptism for service,' dropped out, or rarely been able to get a general hold upon Methodism? Because experience, the great trier of all doctrines, theories and suppositions, has found that the profession of entire sanctification as an instantaneous work does not stand the test of reality. As a general theory, it does not work. People who profess it soon find they are subject to the same temptations that Christians generally have, and members who are 'entirely sanctified' do not display greater wisdom or piety than those who are not."

Dr. Rowe faces the issue squarely as to the teaching of John Wesley and the early Methodists concerning holiness as an instantaneous epochal experience coming subsequent to regeneration. He does not fall into the blunder of some eminent modern writers in spending much time and effort in an endeavor to prove that Mr. Wesley was mixed up in his teaching, and taught two separate theories conecrning holiness, and that in the latter years of his life he weakened in his emphasis on holiness. Dr. Rowe's statements also leave no doubt as to the position of the early Methodist leaders. The records are clear, as in the case of Francis Asbury, that holiness is an instantan-

WESLEY'S HEART-WARMING RELIGION 43

eous work of grace subsequent to regeneration, was a dominant doctrine in the preaching and teaching of the early Methodist leaders.

We are, however, surprised when Dr. Rowe says: "Entire sanctification as an instantaneous work does not stand the test of reality." He quoted Mr. Wesley as writing toward the end of his life: "We are still 'compassed about with a great cloud of witnesses:' " As to the testimony to the reality of sanctification as an instantaneous work, and then follows within a few paragraphs with his own statement: " . . Entire sanctification as an instantaneous work does not stand the test of reality." When evaluating the statements of Mr. Wesley and Dr. Rowe, it seems only fair to raise the question: Who has "at hand quantity in data", for forming the more accurate conclusion, Mr. Wesley or Dr. Rowe? We believe that Mr. Wesley had "at hand quantity in data," which would give his statement precedence in most any court where evidence is weighed.

If "entire sanctification as an instantaneous work does not stand the test of reality" what about "a cloud of witnesses" whose testimony cannot with any degree of fairness be questioned, which is to the fact that this experience does stand the test of reality? What about Francis Asbury and Wm. McKendree? What about the host of other Methodist bishops who have witnessed to this experience standing the "test of reality?" What about Frances E. Willard? What about General Wm. Booth and the Salvation Army? What about Dwight L. Moody, and Charles G. Finney, who both witnessed to being baptized with the Holy Ghost subsequent to regeneration. What about Hudson Taylor, the founder of the China Inland Mission? What about the late Lizzie H. Glide, who was properly designated as "the most philanthropic woman in world Methodism"?

I was the pastor of this remarkable woman during the closing ten years of her life and she told me repeatedly that her sanctification as an instantaneous work of grace following her regeneration, was the beginning of her world wide program of Christian philanthropy. Until these testimonies along with an innumerable host of others are invalidated, the statement that " . . . entire sanctification as an instantaneous work does not stand the test of reality" must remain challenged.

The Interpretation of Wesley's Position By Another Eminent Theologian

Dr. Wm. R. Cannon, Dean of the Candler School of Theology of Emory University, in his book, "The Theology of John Wesley," gives the following analysis of Wesley's doctrine of sanctification:

"Perfection, in Wesley's own words, is nothing more nor less than 'that habitual disposition of the soul, which(in sacred writings, is termed holiness; and which directly implies, the being cleansed from sin, 'from all filthiness both of flesh and spirit;' and, by consequence, the being endued with those virtues which were also in Christ Jesus; the being so 'renewed in the spirit of our mind,' as to be 'perfect as our father in heaven is perfect.'

"Or, put it another way:

"Here, then is the sum of the perfect law; this is

the true circumcision of the heart. Let the spirit return to God that gave it, with the whole train of its affections. 'Unto the place from whence all the rivers came,' thither let them flow again. Other sacrifices from us we would not; but the living sacrifice of the heart he hath chosen. Let it be continually offered up to God through Christ, in flames of holy love. . . . Let your soul be filled with an entire love of him, that you may love nothing but for his sake.

"Perfection is the completion of the development of sanctification begun at regeneration. There man is given power over outward sin, and love becomes the dominating motive of his life. But, tho love dominates in all its dealings with other men and is the guide of all his actions, it is not the only motive of his life; and he is tormented by the urges, cravings, and dispositions of his old nature, by evil thoughts and suggestions which furnish the occasion for returning to open sin. However, when the Christian reaches the state of entire sanctification, when he attains the goal of perfection, these wrong tempers are taken away, the dispositions which trouble him are made to vanish, and the craving and urge after wrong which by grace he has kept in subjection, no longer remain in his soul. Love has entire possession of him.

"Christian perfection, for Wesley, means therefore, only one thing, and that is purity of motives: the love of God, freed entirely from all the corruptions of natural desire and emancipated completely from any interest in self or in any other person or thing apart from God, guides unhindered every thought and every action of a man's life. In body and mind, the perfect Christian is still finite; he makes mistakes in judgment as long as he lives; these mistakes in judgment occasion mistakes in practice, and mistakes in practice often have bad moral consequences. Thus perfection in the sense of infallibility does not exist on the face of the earth. (The Theology of John Wesley. P. 240, 241).

Sanctification May Come In A Moment

"But how, we ask, is Christian perfection to be achieved? How long do we have to continue in the moral struggle, fighting temptation and by grace keeping our natural passions in subjection? What can we do to win this priceless gift? To this Wesley answers by saying that perfection is not achieved by effort; there is not a single moral act that a man can perform to win it. Like justification, it comes by faith and is the free gift of God. All we can do is continue patiently in the faith that is given us, remain loyal morally and spiritually, and steadfastly believe that what God has promised he will perform. In fact, in his sermons on 'The Scriptural Way of Salvation,' Wesley indicates that if we sincerely believe that God will do it, then it is reasonable for us to expect him to do it at any moment. 'Look for it then every day, every hour, every moment! Why not this hour, this moment? Certainly you may look for it now, if you believe it is by faith.' Does this mean that perfection, entire sanctification, is instantaneous, comes in a moment? Wesley replies that the act of faith wherein perfection is finally wrought in the soul, does come in a moment, just as in the case of justification; but a gradual work precedes that moment, so that sanctification, considered as a whole, is a process of development which begins at the very moment a person is justified. Often the act of perfection seems itself to be gradual, and not instantaneous, in that the person in whom it is wrought does not know the particular moment in which all his sinful urges cease to be; but, 'it is often difficult to perceive the instant in which a man dies; yet there is an instant in which life ceases. And if ever sin ceases, there must be a last moment of its existence, and a first moment of our deliverance from it.'

"It must be remarked at this point that perfection, or the rule for perfect love supreme, is not in Wesley's thought a static state with no further progress and development. Tho it is true that he does not succeed in explaining the nature of spiritual development beyond perfection, he does himself raise the question: 'Is it improvable?' and he answers: 'It is so far from lying in an indivisible point, from being incapable of increase, that one perfected in love may grow in grace far swifter than he did before'." (The Theology of John Wesley, pp. 242, 243).

Perfect Love In Complete Control

"Thus there is no further development in which dispositions which trouble us and furnish the occasion for the return to open sin are gradually being overcome. Perfect love is in complete control. And yet there are new occasions always for the demonstration of love and thus for the enrichment of life. These are the means of growth in grace. It is a pity that

Wesley did not have access to A. E. Taylor's notion of 'A possibility which combines attainment and aspiration and which leaves room in a society of just men made perfect for a very real and intense moral life.' This is exactly the idea that Wesley is trying to get across in his emphasis on growth in grace subsequent even to entire sanctification. It must be noted here, also, that Wesley believed that a man can fall from the state of entire sanctification and be lost. Everything depends on his own freedom in willing to remain in any spiritual state in which God by his faith has placed him. 'I do not,' Wesley writes, 'include an impossibility of falling from it, either in part or in whole.'

"Christian perfection, or full sanctification, is 'the grand depositum which God has lodged with the people called Methodists; and for the sake of propagating this chiefly he appeared to have raised us up.' It is the end of which justification is the beginning—the final goal toward which all ethical development moves." (The Theology of John Wesley, by Cannon. P. 242, 243).

Wesley Maintains His Position to the End

John Wesley did not shift from his major emphasis upon sanctification toward the close of his life as some would seek to make it appear. Sanctification was a major emphasis with Mr. Wesley until the close of his earthly pilgrimage. The late Dr. H. C. Morrison in an editorial in The Pentecostal Herald, bearing date of Sept. 15, 1937, quotes some very striking statements from John Wesley, toward the closing years

WESLEY'S HEART-WARMING RELIGION

of his life, which statements we give in the following paragraphs. Six years before his death Mr. Wesley wrote Rev. Freeborn Garretson, saying: "It will be well, as soon as any of them find peace with God, to exhort them to go on to perfection. The more explicitly and strongly you press all believers to aspire after entire sanctification as obtainable now by simple faith, the more the whole work of God will prosper."

During this same year, 1785, Mr. Wesley wrote Rev. John Oglive: "God will prosper you in your labors, especially if you constantly and strongly exhort all believers to expect full sanctification now by simple faith."

The evidence seems conclusive that John Wesley never changed his view of sanctification as a definite work of grace subsequent to regeneration as some modern leaders have endeavored to set forth in their efforts to discredit the doctrine so universally held by early Methodists.

Under date of September 15, 1790, only five months and 17 days before his death, (See Wesley Vol. 7, p. 153), Mr. Wesley wrote Robert Carr Brackenburg, Esquire: "I am glad Brother D. has more light with regard to full sanctification. This doctrine is the grand depositum which God has lodged with the people called Methodists; and for the sake of propagating this chiefly he appears to have raised us up."

Under date of November 26, 1790, only three months and six days before his death, Mr. Wesley wrote to Adam Clarke: "If we can prove that any of our leaders, either directly or indirectly, speak against it (perfect love), let him be a preacher nor a leader no longer. I doubt whether he should continue in the society, because he that could speak thus in our congregations cannot be an honest man."

Only thirty-one days before his death, Mr. Wesley wrote to Rev. John Booth: "Whenever you have the opportunity of speaking to believers, urge them to go on to perfection. Spare no pains, and God even our God, will give you his blessing." Only four days before his death which occurred March 2, 1791, on February 27th, Mr. Wesley said: "We must be justified by faith, and then go on to full sanctification."

Did Wesley Profess the Experience Which He Proclaimed?

Did Mr. Wesley profess the experience of sanctification? There are those who claim that he did not profess the experience himself. Dr. John Paul, associate editor of The Herald, well known educator and author, in a 1955 issue of The Herald, gives the following timely observation on this question:

" We are asked to answer those learned biographers and journalists who state that John Wesley never professed to have received the blessing of perfect love or holiness, which he expounded so freely. The great James M. Buckley, 32 years Editor of The New York Christian Advocate, included the following words in an article he wrote on that question.

" 'All Wesley's followers assumed him to be what he urged them to be. Before they were in a situation to make record, his position was so fixed that to record this description of his state would have been unthought of. He preached entire sanctification in many public controversies. He urged and defended the profession of it, under certain conditions and safeguards; made lists of professors; told them they had lost it because they did not profess it; and said and did so many things only to be explained upon the assumption that he professed to enjoy the blessing, that no other option can find support.' (Editorial in the New York Christian Advocate, 1914).

"It is my understanding from Wesley's writings about himself that he was born again May 24, 1738, in that Aldersgate meeting where his heart was strangely warmed; and that December 23, 1744, he received what he called the second blessing, or sanctification. Bond's Life of Wesley, pages 114, 115, quotes his journal as follows:

" 'Monday, December 23, 1744, he writes in his journal: 'In the evening while I was reading prayers at Snowsfields, I found such light and strength as I never remember to have had before. . . . Tuesday, 25th, I waked by the grace of God in the same spirit; and about 8, being with two or three that believed in Jesus, I felt such an awe and tender sense of the presence of God as greatly confirmed me therein. So that God was before me all the day long. I sought and found him in every place, and could truly say, when I lay down at night, 'now I have lived a day.' "

Snowsfields: A Great Epoch Similar to Aldersgate

Dr. Olin A. Curtis, in his volume, "The Christian Faith," from which we have already quoted in previ-

52 WESLEY'S HEART-WARMING RELIGION

ous articles makes the following observations concerning Wesley's attainment of the experience of sanctification.

He quotes an entry in John Wesley's Journal, May 14, 1765, which says: "I then saw, in a stronger light than ever before, that only one thing is needful, even faith that worketh by the love of God and man, all inward and outward holiness; and I groaned to love God with all my heart, and to serve him with all my strength."

Following this quotation we find this pertinent paragraph by Dr. Curtis:

"But did Wesley actually reach the experience for which he yearned? In his Journal, December 23-25, 1744, we read this: 'I was unusually lifeless and heavy, till the love feast in the evening; when, just as I was constraining myself to speak, I was stopped, whether I would or no; for the blood gushed out of both my nostrils, so that I could not add another word: but in a few minutes it stayed, and all our hearts and mouths were opened to praise God. Yet the next day I was again as a dead man; but in the evening, while I was reading prayers at Snowsfields, I found such light and strength as I never remember to have had before. I saw every thought as well as every action or word just as it was rising in my heart; and whether it was right before God, or tainted with pride or selfishness. I never knew before (I mean not as at this time) what it was 'to be still before God.' Tuesday, 25. I waked, by the grace of God, in the same spirit; and about eight, being with two or three that believed in Jesus, I felt such an awe and tender sense of the presence

WESLEY'S HEART-WARMING RELIGION 53

of God as greatly confirmed me therein, so that God was before me all the day long. I sought and found him in every place, and could truly say, when I lay down at night, 'Now I have lived a day.' To any one familiar with John Wesley's careful, realistic manner of speech, it is evident that we have here the same sort of testimony to the experience of holiness that we have in his Journal, May 24, 1738, to the experience of conversion. If the one is not quite so near a full definition as the other, it surely is just as expressive of the fact. I find it almost impossible to read Wesley's words in the light of all his later utterance about the doctrine of Christian perfection, and not consider this date, December 24, 1744, as the probable time when he began to love God supremely." (Christian Faith, Curtis. P. 175-176).

No Finality In Perfection

Did John Wesley himself profess the experience of perfect love which he so vigorously claimed and insisted on as a definite experience for Christians, obtainable in this life? There seems to have been no question raised about Wesley himself professing the experience which he proclaimed, by the Methodists of his day, and by his followers for a number of decades succeeding his death.

The choice morsel of evidence for those who deny that Wesley professed the experience of perfect love in a letter from Mr. Wesley, published in Lloyd's Evening Post, London, on April 3, 1767, in which he answered attacks repeatedly made on him by Dr. Dodd, a popular clergyman of London. In this letter Mr. Wes-

54 WESLEY'S HEART-WARMING RELIGION

ley quotes Dr. Dodd as saying: "A Methodist, according to Mr. Wesley, is one who is perfect, and sinneth not in thought, word, or deed. 'Sir, have me excused.' This is not 'according to Mr. Wesley.' I have told all the world I am not perfect; and yet you allow me to be a Methodist. I tell you flat, I have not attained the character I draw." (Wesley's Works, Carlton and Porter, Vol. 4, p. 245).

In evaluating this statement of Mr. Wesley we must bear in mind that he was constantly portraying by pen, sermon and testimony the various stages of Christian experience including the primary stage of justification, a more advanced stage in perfection of love, and a still more advanced stage in perfection in maturity.

When Mr. Wesley said in his letter to Dr. Dodd: "I have not attained the character I draw," he made reference to previous statements in his letter concerning the portrayal of a character which is lifted up as the ideal and the pattern toward which all Christians should be striving. In this previous section of the letter Mr. Wesley says: "Five or six and thirty years ago, I much admired the character of a perfect Christian drawn by Clemens Alexandrinus. Five or six and twenty years ago, a thought came into my mind, of drawing such a character myself, only in a more scriptural manner, and mostly in the very words of the Scripture. This I entitled, 'the character of a Methodist,' believing that curiosity would incite more people to read it, and also that some prejudice might thereby be removed from candid men. . . . To the same effect I speak in the conclusion, 'These are the principles and practices of our sect; these are the marks of a true Methodist; i.e., a true Christian ." (Wesley's Works, Vol. 4, p. 245).

The character which Mr. Wesley portrays he describes as having "the marks of a true Methodist; i.e., a true Christian." It is concerning an ideal character which Mr. Wesley labels as a "true Methodist" and "a true Christian" that he says: "I have not attained the character I draw." The interpretation which holds that these words are a denial on the part of Wesley of having obtained perfect love, must in order to be consistent, also take the position that he denied being "a true Methodist" and "a true Christian". When Wesley said in the letter under discussion: "I have told all the world I am not perfect" he was certainly not denying the attainment of perfect love in this life, but rather stating that he had not attained a finality of perfection in maturity in the Christian life.

"Still Breathing Nothing But Love"

The letter under discussion which is quoted so frequently to prove Wesley did not profess the experience of perfect love is recorded in his journal under date of Thursday, March 26th, 1767. On this same day in which the letter is recorded, we find this entry in his journal: "On Ash Wednesday, March 4, I dined at a friend's with Mr. Whitefield, still breathing nothing but love." (Wesley's Works, Vol. 4, p. 245). These words, "still breathing nothing but love," answer very clearly Wesley's definition of perfect love which he enjoined upon his followers and which he here very clearly professes for himself in the very same entry in his journal in which he says: "I have not attained the character I draw."

It seems quite clear that when Wesley said: "I have not attained the character I draw", he was speaking concerning a finality of perfection in maturity which no Christian should ever profess to have attained. In his sermon on Christian perfection, he interprets the "fathers" in a passage in John's First Epistle, as a type of perfection in maturity. He says: "I write unto you, fathers, because ye have known him that is from the beginning. Ye have known both the father, and the son, and the spirit of Christ, in your inmost soul. Ye are 'perfect men,' being grown up to 'the measure of the stature of the fulness of Christ' ".

Mr. Wesley discusses at length the perfection of maturity in the sermon which he preached on the occasion of the death of the Rev. Mr. John Fletcher, Vicar of Madeley, Stropshire. He used as a text: "Mark the perfect man, and behold the upright: for the end of that man is peace." Psalm 37:37. He describes the perfection of maturity as illustrated in the life of John Fletcher in these words:

"As to his outward behavior, the upright Christian believer is blameless and unreprovable. He is holy, as Christ that called him is holy, in all manner of conversation; ever laboring to have a conscience void of offense, toward God and toward man. He not only avoids all outward sin, but 'abstains from all appearance of evil.' He steadily walks in all the public and private ordinances of the Lord blameless. He is zealous of good works; as he hath time, doing good, in every kind and degree to all men. And in the whole course of his life, he pursues one invariable rule—whether he eats or drinks, or whatever he does, to do all to the glory of God." (Wesley's Works, Vol. 1, p. 522).

In his funeral sermon for Mr. Fletcher, Wesley speaks of the floodtide of peace which comes to the mature Christian in a manner never before known. He says:

"This peace they experienced in a higher or lower degree, (supposed they continued in the faith) from the time they first found redemption in the blood of Jesus, even the forgiveness of sins. But when they have nearly finished their course, it generally flows as a river even in such a degree, as it had not before entered into their hearts to conceive. A remarkable instance of this, out of a thousand, occurred many years ago. Enoch Williams, one of the first of our preachers that was stationed at Cork, (who had received this peace when he was 11 years old, and never lost it for an hour) after he had rejoiced in God with joy unspeakable, during the whole course of his illness, was too much exhausted to speak many words, but just said, 'Peace, peace!' and died.

"So was the scripture fulfilled. But it was far more gloriously fulfilled in the late eminent servant of God; as will appear if we consider a few circumstances, first, of his life, and secondly, in his triumphant death." (Wesley's Works, Vol. 1, pages 522-523).

It was concerning such a perfection of maturity as illustrated in a life like that of John Fletcher, that Wesley spoke, when he said: "I have not attained the character I draw."

While Wesley had not attained the perfection in maturity, which in his thinking was a panorama of increasing glory, corresponding with his increasing capacity for the abounding love of God, he did very definitely profess a perfection in purity of love whereby he testified: 'I dined at a friend's with Mr. Whitefield, still breathing nothing but love."

In another letter to Dr. Dodd than the one from which we have quoted, Mr. Wesley expounds a perfection in love which he definitely claimed to have attained himself along with "many hundred children of God whom I personally know." In the introductory paragraph of this letter Mr. Wesley says: "Whoever, therefore, will give me more light with regard to Christian perfection, will do me a singular favor. The opinion I have concerning it at present, I espouse merely because I think it is scriptural. If therefore I am convinced it is not scriptural, I shall willingly relinquish it." (Wesley's Works, Vol. 6, p. 534).

In this letter Wesley discusses a victory for the Christian whereby sinful and unholy desires are stifled "in the birth". In this discussion he gives a personal testimony concerning a perfection of love which he had attained along with many of his followers. He says:

"Taking my words as they lie in connection thus, (and taken otherwise they are not my words but yours,) I must still aver, they speak both my own experience, and that of many hundred children of God whom I personally know. All this, with abundantly more than this, is contained in that single expression, 'the loving God with all our heart, and serving him with all our strength.' Nor did I ever say or mean any more by perfection, than thus loving and serving God." (Wesley's Works, Vol. 6, p. 535).

The Time And Manner of Receiving Perfect Love

The time and manner of receiving the perfection in love which Mr. Wesley claimed for himself and many of his followers is described by him in these words:

"As to the manner, I believe this perfection is always wrought in the soul by a simple act of faith; consequently, in an instant. But I believe a gradual work, both preceding and following that instant. As to the time, I believe this instant is generally the instant of death . . but I believe it may be ten, twenty, or forty years before. I believe it is usually many years after justification; but that it may be within five years or five months after it, I know no conclusive argument to the contrary." (Wesley's Works, Vol. 9, pages 22, 29, 3rd London edition—Mason, 1830).

In the conference minutes of 1759 this record is given: "Q. What is Christian perfection? A. 1. The loving God with all our heart, mind, soul, and strength; and our neighbor as ourselves, which implies deliverance from all sin: 2. That this is received by faith: 3. That it is given simultaneously, in one moment: 4. That we are to expect it (not at death) but every moment: 5. That now is the accepted time, now is the day of salvation. (Wesley's Works, Vol. 11, p. 369, 3rd London edition—Mason, 1830).

"John Wesley's Personal Experience of Christian Perfection" is the title of an article by Dr. Roy S. Nicholson, in the Asbury Seminarian, issue 1952. Dr. Nicholson makes a significant observation concerning the letter by Mr. Wesley to Dr. Dodd as found in Tyerman's Life and Times of John Wesley and used by Tyerman as a basis of his insistent denial that Wesley ever professed to have the experience of perfect love, or entire sanctification. The letter is still being quoted by numerous modern writers as evidence that Wesley did not profess the experience of perfect love. Dr. Nicholson makes this observation:

"Concerning this letter and the use now made of it, perhaps it will be well to bear in mind that Wesley lived 24 years after it was published. In so far as can be ascertained, he was never called in question by a colleague or the conference over it, nor did he deem it needful to offer any explanation for it in his writings. None of his contemporaries who wrote an account of his life and times felt it needful to mention, explain, or otherwise account for the statement. Insofar as is known to this writer, Tyerman, who published his works more than a century after the letter appeared in print, is the first to use it as proof that Wesley disclaimed Christian perfection as a personal experience. It is apparent that Wesley, his followers, and his critics understood what he meant and were satisfied with his explanation." (The Asbury Seminarian, pages 83, 84, 1952 issue).

A Passionate Plea

The urgency with which Mr. Wesley insisted upon sanctification for believers, is clearly revealed in a passionate plea in the closing of his sermon; "The Scriptural Way of Salvation." He says:

"But does God work this great work in the soul gradually or instantaneously? Perhaps it may be gradually wrought in some; I mean in this sense, they do not advert to the particular moment wherein sin ceases to be. But it is infinitely desirable, were it the will of God that it should be done instantaneously; that the Lord should destroy sin 'by the breath of his mouth,' in a moment, in the twinkling of an eye. And so he generally does; the plain fact, of which there is evidence enough to satisfy any unprejudiced person. Now therefore look for it every moment! Look for it in the way above described; in all those good works whereunto thou art 'created anew in Christ Jesus.' There is no danger; you can be worse, if you are no better for that expectation. For were you to be disappointed of your hope, still you lose nothing but you shall not be disappointed of your hopes: it will come, and will not tarry. Look for it then every day, every hour, every moment! Why not this hour, this moment? Certainly you may look for it now, if you believe it is by faith. And by this token you may surely know whether you seek it by faith or by works. If by works, you want something to be done first, before you are sanctified. You think, I must first be or do thus or thus. Then you are seeking it by works unto this day. If you seek it by faith, you may expect it as you are; and if as you are, then expect it now. It is of importance to observe, that there is an inseparable connection between these three points, expected by faith, expected as you are, expected now! To deny one of them is to deny them all. To allow one is to allow them all. Do you believe we are sanctified by faith? Be true then to your principles; and look for this blessing just as you are, neither better nor worse; as a poor sinner that has still nothing to pay, nothing to plead, but that Christ died. And if you look for it as you are, then expect it now. Stay for nothing: why should you? Christ is ready; and he is all you want. He is waiting for you: He is at the door! Let your inmost soul cry out,

> 'Come in, come in, thou heavenly guest!
> Nor hints again remove;
> But sup with me, and let the feast
> Be everlasting love.' "

A Living Sacrifice

The urgent plea of Mr. Wesley to all believers was to enter in to the experience of sanctification, now. It was right and proper for him to make such a plea, for we find the same urgency in the holy scriptures concerning the offering up of ourselves "as a living sacrifice, holy, acceptable unto God, which is our reasonable service." There need be no delay for God's sanctifying grace in your heart. He is more anxious to sanctify you than you are to be sanctified. He has made every provision for you that you might be sanctified wholly thru the merits of the shed blood of his son Jesus Christ. Bear in mind that he not only died that the world might be saved, but he likewise died that all believers might be sanctified wholly. This was the burden of the prayer of the great apostle to the Gentiles as he prayed for the Thessalonian Christians: "And the very God of peace sanctify you wholly; and I pray God your whole spirit and soul and body be preserved blameless unto the coming of our Lord Jesus Christ. Faithful is he that calleth you, who also will do it." (I Thess. 5:23, 24).

The Lord will not disappoint you, if you heed his invitation and place everything upon the altar for time and for eternity. His promises are true. He has never failed in the fulfillment of any promise when the conditions of the promise have been met. He has never turned any earnest seeking heart away who has come seeking the fulness of his saving power. He has said: "Him that cometh unto me I will in no wise cast out."

God has called us unto holiness. He says in his word: "God hath not called us unto uncleanness, but unto holiness." When you heed his call, he will not disappoint you. When all is placed upon the altar, we have the promise that he accepts the consecration which we bring and the altar sanctifies the gift. There is a step of faith for you to take when you place all upon the altar. That step of faith is to believe that Christ does what he says he does when you consecrate all. He says that when you yield all into his hands unreservedly, he does accept the offering that we bring and he sanctifies the gift which we offer to him, which is ourselves, in utter completeness. "Faithful is he that calleth you, who also will do it." He sanctifies you the moment that you consecrate all, and believe. Make your consecration now, and then say to him out of a heart of trust and faith: "Oh Lord I do believe, that thou dost sanctify, even me."

Made in the USA
Columbia, SC
12 January 2025